BRANCH LINE TO ILFRACOMBE

Vic Mitchell and Keith Smith

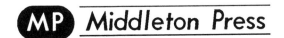

MP Middleton Press

First published October 1993

ISBN 1 873793 21 9

© Middleton Press 1993

Design - Deborah Goodridge
Typesetting - Barbara Mitchell
Deborah Goodridge

Published by Middleton Press
Easebourne Lane
Midhurst
West Sussex
GU29 9AZ
Tel: (0730) 813169
(From 16 April 1995 - (01730) 813169)

Printed & bound by Biddles Ltd,
Guildford and Kings Lynn

CONTENTS

ACKNOWLEDGEMENTS

In addition to those mentioned in the photographic credits, we have received great assistance from P.G.Barnes, G.Croughton, S.P.Derek, M.King, J.R.W.Kirkby, N.Langridge, A.Ll.Lambert, Mr.D. and Dr.S.Salter, N.Stanyon, E.Youldon and our wives. To all these we express our deep gratitude.

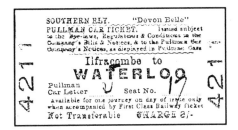

Railways of the Exmoor area in 1935.
(Railway Magazine)

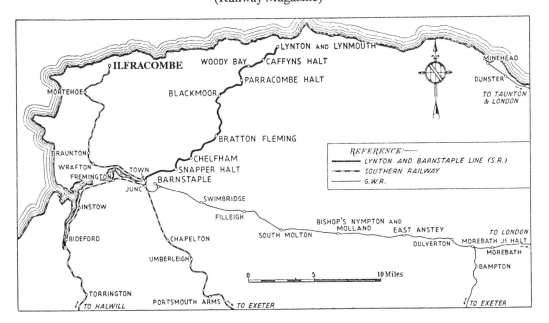

The 1" to 1 mile map of 1938 has the GWR's Victoria Road terminus below the word *BARNSTAPLE*. In the lower right corner is the connection between the GWR and the SR and lower left is the line to Torrington.

GEOGRAPHICAL SETTING

The route crossed the tidal River Taw at Barnstaple and followed its north bank closely for three miles after crossing the south flowing River Yeo. The valley broadens and gives sufficient level ground between the railway and the water for an airfield, RAF Chivenor. Nearby is Wrafton, the line curving northwards here towards Braunton where it entered the narrow valley of the River Caen. At this station, a severe climb commenced. For nearly five miles the track was inclined at mostly 1 in 40 to Mortehoe, the summit at over 600ft above sea level.

In this vicinity the railway was built on fragmented limestones which give unstable cliffs (and cuttings). There followed a winding descent of three miles, much at 1 in 36, to the coastal resort of Ilfracombe, situated in a small cliff-enclosed bay on the north coast of Devon.

The maps in this volume are to the scale of 25" to 1 mile, unless otherwise indicated.

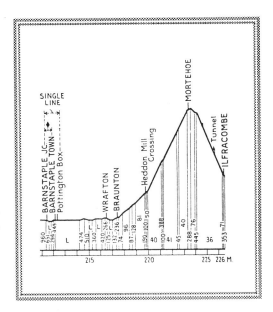

HISTORICAL BACKGROUND

The horse-worked Taw Vale Railway carried mineral traffic between Barnstaple and Fremington from 25th April 1848.

On 1st August 1854 broad gauge trains began to operate from Crediton to Barnstaple and on to Fremington, using the former mineral route. Extension to Bideford and to Exeter took place in 1855. In 1862 the London & South Western Railway leased the line and soon laid a third rail for its standard gauge trains.

After Ilfracombe had sought a railway for many years, with much acrimony and some rioting, the Barnstaple and Ilfracombe Railway Company obtained an Act of Parliament on 4th July 1870. By this time the town was well established as a somewhat exclusive holiday resort, patrons arriving by paddle steamer from Bristol, Portishead and towns in South Wales.

The opening of the railway on 20th July 1874 heralded a further period of growth for Ilfracombe and prosperity for the district. The LSWR operated the line (a Light Railway) from the outset and absorbed the company in 1875. Increase in traffic necessitated the doubling of most of the single line between 1888 and 1891.

The LSWR was a constituent of the Southern Railway when it was formed in 1923 and became part of the Southern Region of British Railways upon nationalisation in 1948. It was transferred to the Western Region on 1st January 1963, although it had been under that region's commercial administration between 1950 and 1958.

Goods traffic ceased on 5th September 1964, the track was singled on 17th December 1967, and complete clos re followed on 5th October 1970. A subsequent attempt by the North Devon Railway Co. Ltd. to acquire the line failed, investors sadly losing money. The remaining track was lifted in 1975.

PASSENGER SERVICES

The table below indicates the number of down trains per day for selected years and, when compared with the corresponding table in our *Exeter to Barnstaple* album, reveals that for most of the first half of this century there were about twice as many trains on the branch than the main line. (The LSWR considered Ilfracombe to be on a branch but the SR regarded Torrington as on the lesser route). The figures indicate the importance of local traffic, although many trains started from Waterloo.

	Weekdays	Sundays
1870	4	-
1889	7	2
1906	15	2
1914	13	3
1924	14	3
1934	17	8
1944	11	4
1954	13	7
1963	11	5
1970	5	3

The timetables for winter Sundays often showed fewer or no trains but those for summer Saturdays were greatly enhanced, except during the war years.

From 1889 the GWR operated through trains or coaches from Paddington via their Taunton-Barnstaple route, but an agreement with the LSWR in 1910 resulted in the pooling of receipts, and although serious competition ended, through facilities continued. Prior to World War I Ilfracombe also received through trains from Bradford via the Midland Railway and Templecombe, and also from Leeds via the Great Central Railway and Oxford.

Almost all trains ran the full length of the branch but there was one short working between Ilfracombe and Mortehoe on weekdays in some years before both World Wars.

In the 1950s there was an increased number of through trains from Taunton, including one on weekday mornings which terminated at Mortehoe. During this decade there were regular through trains from Wolverhampton, Manchester and Portsmouth.

The introduction of a full DMU service in September 1964 resulted in through workings from Exmouth, Sidmouth, Honiton and Salisbury but Waterloo direct services ceased. The "Devon Belle" and "Atlantic Coast Express" are discussed in captions 18 and 87.

October 1944 London through trains.

Summer 1951 through trains.

LOCOMOTIVES

After trials with other engines, the LSWR decided to order three 0-6-0s from Beyer, Peacock & Co. The type had a low axle weight to suit the light track, small diameter wheels for the exceptionally steep gradients and a good performance record in Sweden. The three arrived in 1873 and a further five followed. They became known as the "Ilfracombe Goods", although they worked all services on the branch. On the gradients trains were restricted to four coaches and a van or eight wagons and a van. After the track was relaid at the time of the doubling most of the engines were transferred for goods work elsewhere, and six were later bought by Mr.H.F.Stephens for use on Light Railways under his control.

"Jubilee" class A12 0-4-2s displaced the "Ilfracombe Goods" on passenger work on the branch and class T1 0-4-4Ts were in use for many years around the turn of the century. From about 1914, class M7 0-4-4Ts were commonly used on the branch.

The SR introduced their new class N 2-6-0s in 1925 on trains running to Exeter or beyond, these predominating until the introduction of the "West Country" class in 1945.

The first 2-6-2Ts of LMS design arrived at Barnstaple in 1953 and were used on the Torrington-Halwill Junction route. They increased in number and were eventually used on most local services. Class 4 2-6-4Ts made occasional appearances in the final years of steam.

After the advent of DMUs in 1964, the few remaining locomotive hauled holiday trains were worked mostly by "Warship" Type 4 diesels.

Most of the GWR classes of locomotive to work the branch are illustrated in this album.

1. "Ilfracombe Goods" no. 324 of 1875 survived on the Shropshire & Montgomeryshire Railway until 1941, carrying the name *Hesperus*. The first locomotives were supplied with four-wheeled tenders, parallel chimneys and the dome was close to the cab. Other views of members of this class during their second careers can be found in the Middleton Press albums *Branch Line to Shrewsbury, Branch Line to Tenterden* and *East Kent Light Railway.* (Lens of Sutton)

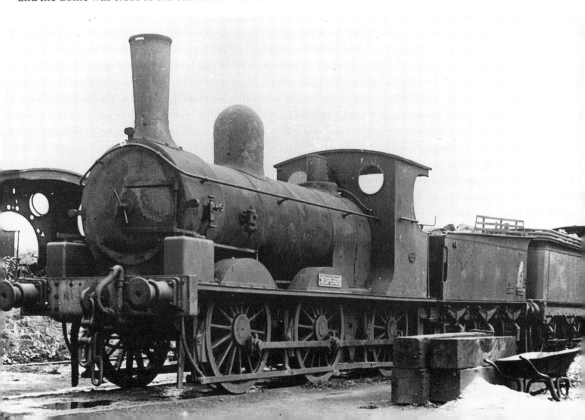

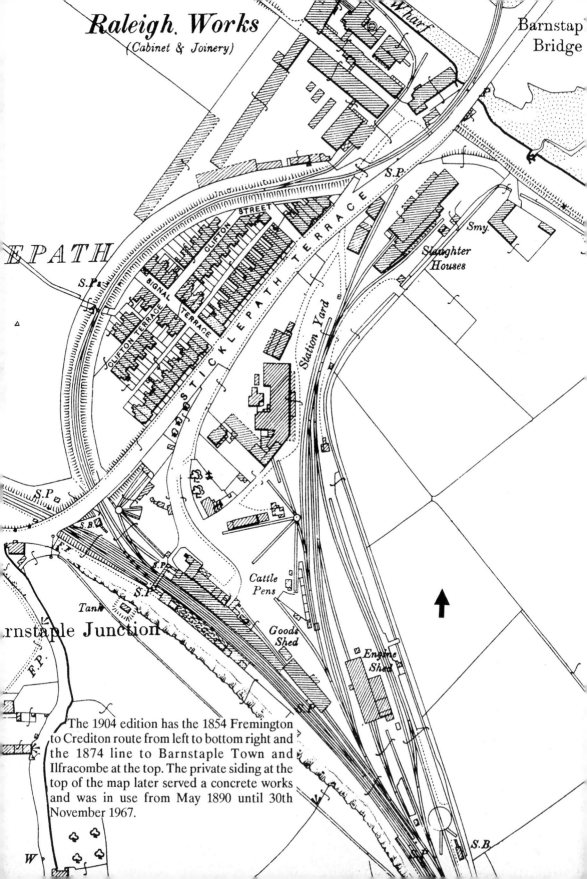

Raleigh. Works
(Cabinet & Joinery)

Barnstap
Bridge

Wharf

RALEIGH PATH

S.P.

CLIFTON STREET

SIGNAL TERRACE

CLIFTON TERRACE

STICKLEPATH TERRACE

Station Yard

Slaughter
Houses

Smy.

S.P.

S.P.

S.B.

Tank

rnstaple Junction

F.P.

Cattle
Pens

Goods
Shed

Engine
Shed

S.B.

W

The 1904 edition has the 1854 Fremington
to Crediton route from left to bottom right and
the 1874 line to Barnstaple Town and
Ilfracombe at the top. The private siding at the
top of the map later served a concrete works
and was in use from May 1890 until 30th
November 1967.

BARNSTAPLE JUNCTION

2.   Until 1874, when the station became a junction, there was only one platform. A down platform was added then and this became an island platform in 1924. It is seen on the left of this August 1935 view, which includes two ex-LBSCR class E1/Rs, no. 2094 (on the middle road) and no. 2696. (H.F.Wheeller)

3.   Class M7 0-4-4Ts nos. 30 and 47 were recorded on 21st July 1925. The goods shed (left) is shown on the right of the previous picture. The shed labourer is clearing ash and clinker, an endless task at all steam depots. The shed number was changed from 72E to 83F on 1st January 1963. (H.C.Casserley)

4. The SR had a financial interest in the Southern National Omnibus Co. Their Bristol no. 190 was providing the service to Lynton on route 110 on 2nd July 1948, the SR's narrow gauge railway to that town having ceased to operate in 1935. (J.H.Aston)

5. New stock to Mr Bulleid's design came into use on the route in 1945, examples of his 3-coach sets and "West Country" class being recorded in the up platform on 20th June 1949. No. 34046 *Braunton* is working the 2.10pm from Ilfracombe. (S.C.Nash)

6. At the coaling stage on 28th September 1956 is class M7 0-4-4T no. 30255. Another M7 and a "West Country" are in the shed. Closure of the former Barnstaple GWR shed in 1952 increased the number of engines serviced here. Closure of Torrington in 1956 raised the number of men to over 100 and the locomotives to about 16, but the end came here in 1964. (H.C.Casserley)

7. A "West Country" stands in the down loop beside the water column awaiting departure to Ilfracombe. In the foreground is the signalman's crossing to the tablet carrier for the Torrington line. (Wessex coll.)

8. The signalman returns to "B" Box with the single line token as no. 31849 clatters into the station on 23rd July 1963 with the 12.15pm from Ilfracombe. (R.Palmer)

9. Smoke engulfs the platform as parcels delivery vans wait in the station forecourt on 15th May 1964. The stone wall segregated passengers from the cattle and other goods train traffic. The architect was William Tite whose station designs for the London & Southampton Railway first impressed the railway world. (R.M.Casserley)

SOUTHERN RAILWAY.
This Ticket is issued subject to the By-laws
Regulations & Conditions stated in the
Company's Time Tables Bills & Notices
Available on day of issue only
BARNSTAPLE TOWN to
BARNSTAPLE G.W
VIA BARNSTAPLE JUNCTION
3rd CLASS   3rd CLASS
Fare 3d   Fare 3d

10. "A" Box was designated "East Box" until 1949 and remained in use until 1st November 1987. The frame had 40 levers and was removed for use at Ropley on the Mid-Hants Railway. Look for the coal stack for the stove and the scythe sharpening. (Wessex coll.)

11. "B" Box was designated "West" until 2nd October 1949. It dated from the track and platform alterations of 1924 and remained in use until 21st May 1971, when the line eastwards was singled and the loop line, along with the centre road, was taken out of use. (Wessex coll.)

Other views and maps of this station are to be found in our *Exeter to Barnstaple* **album.**

12.   On the right is the 1924 footbridge extension and steps which gave direct access to the developing residential area south of the town. Tickets were required only when passing the inspector's hut visible at the end of the platform. (Wessex coll.)

13. The 10.10 Ilfracombe to Exeter rounds the curve on the last day of operation, 3rd October 1970. The lines on the left had closed to passengers on 4th October 1965 but remained in use for clay traffic until 1982. (S.C.Nash)

14. The LSWR's slaughterhouse was situated at the north end of the goods yard, close to the River Taw, into which unwanted fluids found their way. This and the company's other slaughterhouses at Crediton, Copplestone, Eggesford, Halwell Junction, Holsworthy, Lapford and Sampford Courtenay were controlled by the Ministry of Food during WWI and were leased or sold to local organisations in 1920. This example was taken over by the North Devon Co-Operative Society and is seen in 1992. The buildings on the left are in front of the site of the Ilfracombe line; the bus has just crossed Barnstaple Bridge (Longbridge), and the new station approach road is in the foreground. (V.Mitchell)

15. The basic railway leaves Barnstaple at the end of a single line, although a loop is available for use by the engineers. A two-car Sprinter is at the buffer-stops waiting to return to Exeter at 16.18 on 31st July 1993. The fence marked the site of the then recently demolished Red Star parcels office, although the much older wooden goods shed seen in picture 2 was still standing behind the camera. (V.Mitchell)

16.   Viewed from the other side of the road bridge seen in pictures 8 and 13 is the "Exeter Flyer", a special train operated by the Southern Counties Touring Society on 3rd October 1965, a year after the end of regular steam operation. This was a relief train, the first having run on 12th September previous. The rear coach is on the single line from Barnstaple Town. (S.C.Nash)

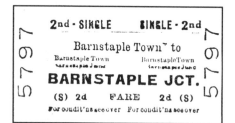

17. Class N no.1857 was recorded with three ex-LSWR coaches prior to the fitting of smoke deflectors to its smokebox. The bridge design was strongly criticised by residents (Barumites) for its ugliness and only a few tears were shed when it was demolished in 1977. (Lens of Sutton)

18. The prestigious "Devon Belle" all Pullman train approaches Barnstaple Town on 16th June 1950, hauled by no. 34025 *Whimple*. When introduced in June 1947 the train left Waterloo at 12.00 noon with four cars for Plymouth and eight for Ilfracombe, which included an observation car. The latter portion was more usually six although ten at peak times was common. The train ran on extended summer weekends only, with a reduced programme of journeys from 1952 until withdrawn at the end of the summer of 1954. The Plymouth portion was dropped in September 1949. (J.J.Smith)

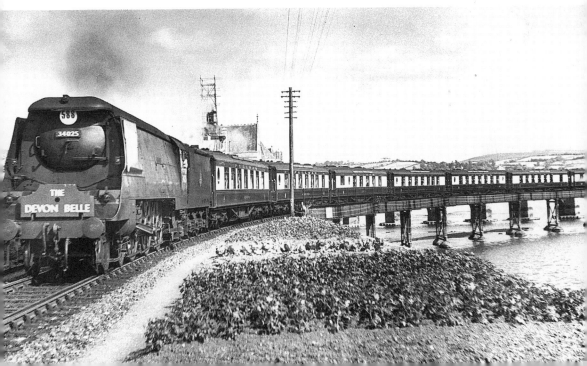

19.   Class N no. 31844 approaches the north bank of the River Taw on 24th June 1960, the train roaring on the ironwork of the bridge which was on a mere seven chain radius. Note the railway's telegraph system attached to the structure. (N.L.Browne)

20.   This part of Barnstaple's waterfront was totally rebuilt when the railway was constructed. The small white building on the left is seen better in the next picture. The North British type 2 is no. D6338. (Wessex coll.)

21.   Road and rail bridges are in the background of this view of the gate box which was not a block post. This crossing linked the quay with The Strand, another being provided only 75yds to the west. (Wessex coll.)

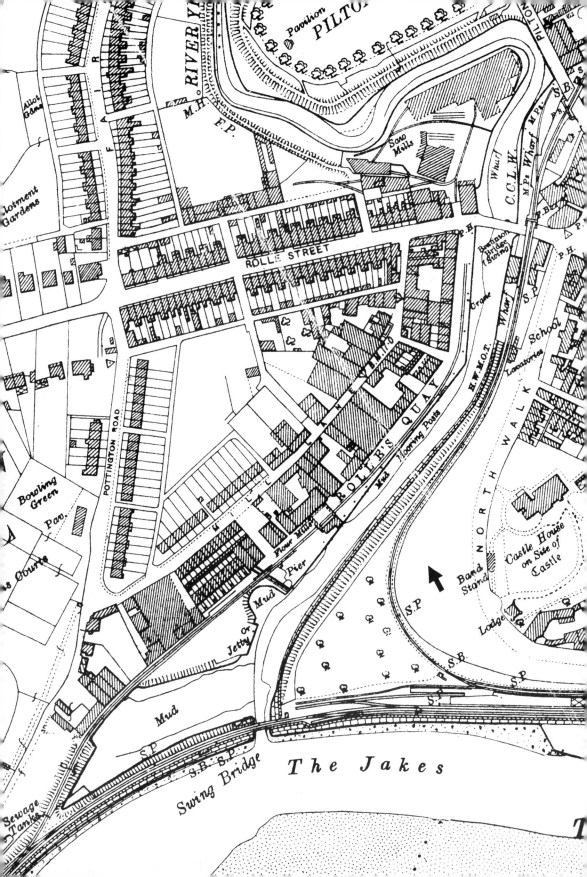

BARNSTAPLE QUAY

22. The first station was at the northern end of the bridge in the area shown in pictures 18 and 21. Its name was changed to "Barnstaple Town" in 1886 and not 1898 as stated in most publications. It closed in that year when a new station was opened 250 yds to the west. A bus station was opened on part of the site in 1922. (North Devon Athaneum)

The 1932 map has the Barnstaple Junction to Ilfracombe line running from bottom right to bottom left. The Lynton & Barnstaple Railway's 2 ft gauge tracks are on the right of the left page and are described in detail in our *Branch Line to Lynton* (Middleton Press).

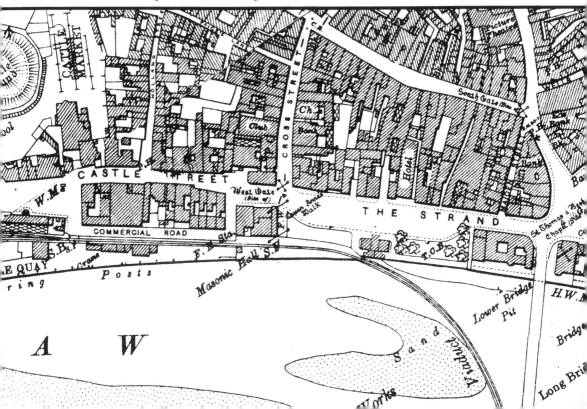

23. The opening of the Lynton & Barnstaple Railway on 16th May 1898 necessitated the provision of a joint station on a new and wider site. There was also space (left) for a goods loop. (Lens of Sutton)

July 1924

EXETER, BARNSTAPLE, BIDEFORD, TORRINGTON, and ILFRACOMBE.—Southern.

Down.	Week Days.	Sundays.
Mls from Exeter		
162 London (W.)....dep.		
162 Salisbury .... "		
Exeter (Queen St.).dep.		
" (St. David's)....		
5 Newton St. Cyres......		
7½ Crediton		
11¾ Yeoford		
14 Copplestone		
15½ Morchard Road......		
18½ Lapford		
22 Eggesford *		
26 South Molton Road †..		
29 Portsmouth Arms		
33 Umberleigh		
35½ Chapelton		
39½ Barnstaple Jn. arr.		
London (Pad.) dep.		
Barnstaple Junc.dep.		
42½ Fremington		
46½ Instow		
43½ Bideford **		
54 Torrington .... arr.		
London (Pad.) dep.		
Barnstaple Junc...dep.		
49½ Barnstaple { arr.		
Town (below) { dep.		
44½ Wrafton		
45½ Braunton §		
51½ Mortehoe ‖		
54½ Ilfracombe ...... arr.		

A Except Sunday nights. Via Eastleigh.
B Leaves at 10 aft. on Sundays.
H Via Exeter (St. David's).
J Luncheon Car to Exeter.
K Luncheon Car to Ilfracombe.
L Luncheon and Tea Cars to Exeter.

R Restaurant Cars to Exeter.
T By Slip Carriage.

BIDEFORD AND CLOVELLY.—
Southern Railway Motor Bus leaves
Bideford at 10 50 mrn. and 4 15 aft.,
arriving Clovelly at 11 50 mrn. and
5 15 aft. respectively.

24. A May 1925 record shows wagons lettered L&BR although the SR had taken control of that line in 1923. On the left are the catch points of the goods loop, which seems almost full. (R.Carpenter coll.)

July 1924

ILFRACOMBE, TORRINGTON, BIDEFORD, BARNSTAPLE and EXETER.—Southern.

(A dense period railway timetable for "Up" trains, with Week Days and Sundays columns. Principal stations listed include: Ilfracombe dep., Mortehoe, Braunton, Wrafton, Barnstaple arr., Town dep., Barnstaple Junc. arr., London (Pad) arr.; Torrington dep., Bideford, Instow, Fremington, Barnstaple J. arr., London (Pad) arr.; Barnstaple Junc. dep., Chapelton, Umberleigh, Portsmouth Arms, South Molton Road, Eggesford, Lapford, Morchard Road, Copplestone, Yeoford, Crediton, Newton St. Cyres, Exeter (St. David's) arr., (Queen St.) arr., Salisbury arr., London (Wat.).)

Notes:
- **A** Via Eastleigh.
- **B** Luncheon Car, Exeter to London.
- **F** Will not convey Passengers for Mortehoe from Ilfracombe from July 28th to September 12th inclusive, except on Saturdays. On Saturdays it will not convey Passengers from Ilfracombe for Stations East of Yeoford.
- **H** Via Exeter (St. David's).
- **K** Passengers cross the town from Barnstaple Junction to Barnstaple (G.W.).
- **N** Restaurant Car, Exeter to London.
- **R** Tea and Dining Car from Exeter.
- **T** Dining Car, Exeter to London.
- **V** Stops to take up only.

CLOVELLY AND BIDEFORD.—
Southern Railway Motor Bus leaves Clovelly at 9 20 mrn. and 3 aft., arriving Bideford at 10 20 mrn. and 4 aft.

- * Station for Chulmleigh (1½ miles).
- † Station for Chulmleigh (2½ miles).
- ‡ Over ½ mile to Barnstaple Station.
- § Station for Saunton Sands.
- ‖ Station for Woolacombe and Lee (Devon).
- ¶ About 1 mile to G.W. Station.
- ** Station for Westward Ho! (3 miles), Appledore (3 miles), Clovelly (11 miles), and Hartland (13 miles).

25. Looking in the opposite direction we see a Lynton-bound train with 2-6-2T no. 761 *Taw* and a coal wagon lettered SR. The raincoated gentleman largely obscures the level crossing gates. (Lens of Sutton)

26. Exchange sidings were provided for the transfer of goods between the gauges. Occasionally locomotives arrived here, such as no. E188 *Lew* when new on 30th July 1925. Other locomotives were transferred here for overhaul at Eastleigh Works. The standard gauge siding remained in place until April 1940. (H.C.Casserley)

27. The line to Lynton closed on 29th September 1935, this photograph having been taken the following year. The exchange sidings are between the two signal posts and

Pottington signal box is in the left distance. It is seen more closely in picture 36.
(R.K.Cope/R.Carpenter coll.)

28. To the right of the row of parked cars is Town station and the site of the former L&BR tracks. Left of centre is the former Corporation electricity works together with the base of its square-section chimney. Its coal supply was landed at Castle Quay (right) and carted across the railway, the SR deriving no business from this source.
(H.C.Casserley coll.)

29. The signal box was at the east end of the platform and is obscured by the canopy in the previous view. The lower quadrant signal is on a typical LSWR lattice post. (Wessex coll.)

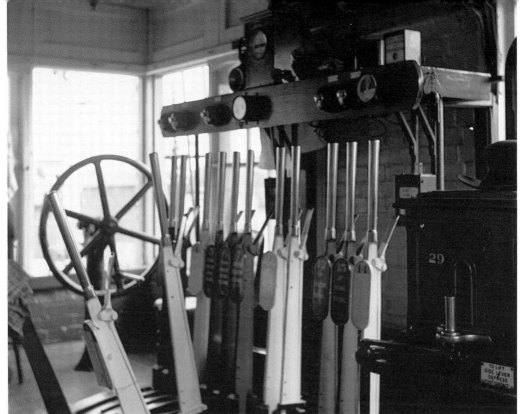

30. Serving as the only intermediate block post on the single line section, the box could be very busy, particularly as the wheel controlled the gates on the road to Castle Quay. (Wessex coll.)

31. On the right is the up starting signal, already seen in picture 29. The main feature is the array of down signals, the small arm being for the goods loop. No public goods facilities were available at this station. (Wessex coll.)

32.   Despite the proximity of the DC power station, station lighting was by gas to the end, which appears to be nigh. The area is now occupied by flats and the part in the background is the site of the Civic Centre. (Lens of Sutton)

34. The station building became an Indian restaurant, which has been extended across the platform, left. The signal box, seen in April 1992, was converted to a L&BR museum and bookshop and was open on weekdays from Easter to October. (V.Mitchell)

33. While this station could have been more usefully retained as the terminus of the line from Exeter, it was just boarded up despite its proximity to the business centre and bus station. Many buses turn at the roundabout shown in picture 14 but passengers are expected to walk over the bridge! (Lens of Sutton)

Barnstaple Town	1928	1936
No. of passenger tickets issued	79496	32745
No. of season tickets issued	21	314
No. of tickets collected	149034	74269
No. of telegrams	819	28
Parcels forwarded	7351	4183
Parcels received	464	381
Horses forwarded	-	-
Milk forwarded - cans 1928/gallons 1936	-	69
Milk received - cans 1928/gallons 1936	-	-
General goods forwarded (tons)	-	-
General goods received (tons)	-	-
Coal, Coke etc.	-	-
Other minerals forwarded	-	-
Other minerals received	-	-
Trucks livestock forwarded	-	-
Trucks livestock received	-	-
Lavatory pennies	8856	3538

WEST OF BARNSTAPLE TOWN

35. At the west end of the goods loop was the swing bridge over the River Yeo, the 59 ft long span being visible beyond the second telegraph pole. The up train is hauled by N class no. 1832, which is on the points to the exchange siding. After its demise, the points were retained for trap purposes. (D.Cullum coll.)

Final summer timetable (Mondays to Fridays).

Exeter to Okehampton, Barnstaple and Ilfracombe

Miles																								
0	EXETER CENTRAL	d			08f03			10c21						13 16	13 16	14 50		14e50	16 56		17 42		19g11	
¾	EXETER ST. DAVID'S	a			08f06			10c25						13 20	13 20	14 54		14e54	17 00		17 45		19g14	
		d	04 05	04 17	08 24		08 45	10 40		11 23				13 35	13 45	15 28		16 00	17 36		17 46		19 45	20 36
5	NEWTON ST CYRES	d					08 52	10 47								15 35			17 43		17 54		19 52	
7¾	CREDITON	d	04 16	04 28	08 34		08 58	10 53		11 34				13 46	13 55	15 41		16 12	17 49		18 00		19 58	20 47
11¼	YEOFORD	d			08 41		09 05	11 00		11 41					14 02	15 48		16 19	17 56		18 07		20 05	20 54
16	BOW	d			08 50			11 09							14 11	15 57			18 05				20 14	
19½	NORTH TAWTON	d			08 57			11 15							14 18	16 03			18 11				20 20	
22	SAMPFORD COURTENAY	d			09 02			11 21							14 23	16 09			18 17				20 26	
25¾	OKEHAMPTON (FOR BUDE Z)	a		04 54	09 10			11 29							14 31	16 17			18 25				20 34	
14½	COPPLESTONE	d					09 11											16 24			18 12			
15¾	MORCHARD ROAD	d					09 15											16 28			18 16			
18¼	LAPFORD	d	04 33				09 20			11 54				14 04				16 33			18 21			21 07
22	EGGESFORD	d					09 28			12 02				14 11				16b43			18 29			21 15
26	KING'S NYMPTON	d					09 34			12 08				14 18				16 49			18 35			21 21
29	PORTSMOUTH ARMS	d					09 40											16 55			18 41			
33	UMBERLEIGH	d	04 57				09 46			12 19				14 29				17 02			18 47			21 32
35¼	CHAPELTON	d					09 51											17 06			18 52			
39¾	BARNSTAPLE JUNCTION (FOR BIDEFORD Z)	a	05 08				09 59			12 30				14 40				17 15			19 00			21 43
		d	05 21				10 02							14 42				17 20			19 03			
40½	BARNSTAPLE TOWN	d	05 25				10 06							14 46				17 24			19 07			
44¼	WRAFTON	d	05 33				10 13							14 53				17 31			19 14			
45¾	BRAUNTON	d	05 37				10 17							14 57				17 35			19 18			
51½	MORTEHOE & WOOLACOMBE	d	05 52				10 31							15 11				17 50			19 32			
54¾	ILFRACOMBE	a	06 00				10 39							15 19				17 58			19 40			

36. Pottington signal box locked the bolts on the swing bridge, was the end of the single line section from Barnstaple Junction, and controlled access to the Rolles Quay siding. It was reduced to a ground frame to lock the bridge on 17th December 1967. Near the house on the left is a ground frame for a crossover near the trailing siding from the down line to Rolles Quay, the gates for which are in line with the left corner of the signal box. (Wessex coll.)

37.   Ships of up to 250 tons could pass the swing bridge into the River Yeo, some carrying timber, ballast and coal to Pilton Wharf, near Braunton Swing Bridge, but most traffic was grain to Stanbury's Mill. The siding runs along the quay - see map by picture 22. (N.W.Hearn coll.)

38.   The mill was built in 1898 and probably generated considerable rail revenue from grain inwards, and flour and other finished products outwards. A partially sheeted LSWR wagon is on the right. The siding was closed on 7th September 1964. (N.W.Hearn coll.)

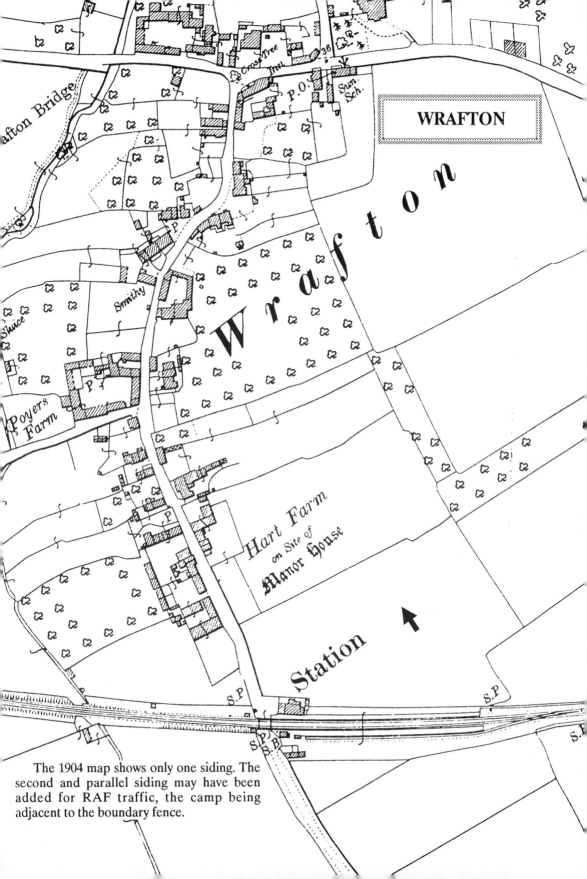

The 1904 map shows only one siding. The second and parallel siding may have been added for RAF traffic, the camp being adjacent to the boundary fence.

39. A view towards Ilfracombe shows the line beginning to curve towards a northerly direction. Both sidings are included, the later one accommodating a camping coach. (A.F.E.Field)

40. Coach 13 was providing lucky holiday-makers with cheap accommodation in the summer of 1948. The water supply is on wheels by the gate, complete with hand pump. By 1960 the tariff was £6 per week in low season rising to £10.10s.0d in the summer months for a 6-berth coach, plus 15s0d for gas - toilets on the station. (J.H.Aston)

41. The buildings provided adequate facilities for passengers from the nearby small village but the RAF personnel may have strained them. Some believe the name to have been derived from the RAF unaware that the village is of great antiquity. (Wessex coll.)

Wrafton	1928	1936
No. of passenger tickets issued	4080	1353
No. of season tickets issued	-	-
No. of tickets collected	4090	1380
No. of telegrams	51	-
Parcels forwarded	235	225
Parcels received	215	279
Horses forwarded	-	-
Milk forwarded - cans 1928/gallons 1936	1527	6567
Milk received - cans 1928/gallons 1936	-	8629
General goods forwarded (tons)	162	220
General goods received (tons)	428	225
Coal, Coke etc.	260	71
Other minerals forwarded	172	215
Other minerals received	6610	34
Trucks livestock forwarded	-	-
Trucks livestock received	-	-
Lavatory pennies	-	-

42. The box ceased to be a block post and was reduced to a ground frame on 17th December 1967 when the line was singled. The down distant was the only colour light signal on the branch. The frame had 17 levers, two of which were spare, and a gate wheel was provided. (Wessex coll.)

43. The rails from the down track have gone but both buffer stops are still in place, the goods yard having closed on 7th September 1964. No. D821 *Greyhound* was of the "Warship" class 42. (Wessex coll.)

44. Rails were still in place in the road when the buildings were photographed in July 1993. One crossing gate post and the down starting signal post remained, although the latter had had a signal arm applied to the wrong side of the post. (V.Mitchell)

45. Vellator Crossing was provided with a 7-lever gate box which remained in use, along with its signals, after the singling. The nearby village is now spelt with one "l". (Wessex coll.)

BRAUNTON GATES

46. Doubling of the track from Pottington to Braunton was completed on 4th August 1890. There had been a passing loop here from the outset. Note the fall-face shunt signal in the foreground. (Lens of Sutton)

47. The gate box had five levers, only two of which were used. It was officially renamed "Braunton East Level Crossing" but, as it was south of Caen Street crossing (and a few degrees to the west!), the name seems to have been little used. (Wessex coll.)

BRAUNTON

The 1904 edition has the track layout at its optimum. A new main road was cut through the centre of the village (right) in the 1930s as shown on the 1" to 1 mile map in the introduction.

Parkin's Farm

Smithy Weir

F.B.
S.P

Burial Ground

Congl. Chap.

Bas Lane School

Town Farm

L.B.

F.B.
P.

F.B.

CAEN STREET

WEST CROSS

Cross Farm

Smy.

Station

Caen Br.

S.B.
Br.

CROSS TREE

P.H.

P.H.

Mill Leat

Goods Shed

Lampreys

CHAPEL STREET

S.P.

Horden's Mill (Corn)

Gubbin's Lane

S.B.

Scur Farm

F.P.

S.P.

Mill Stile

STREET

KING'S LANE

R i.

48. A study of the up starting signal includes a pair of gates (right) that once gave vehicular access to the two short down sidings. On the left is the trap point for the up sidings. (Wessex coll.)

49. A water tank is situated beyond the level crossing and close to it was a 48 ft long trailing siding on which banking engines stood prior to attachment to down trains. Having stopped in the station, these trains had to stop again for this to take place. (Lens of Sutton)

50. Another early view shows all sidings to be devoid of catch points. The sidings on the left later had one each and were sometimes used for banking engines. The portal crane on the right had a capacity of 10 tons. (D.Cullum coll.)

51. A goods train stands in the up platform, the general scene giving the impression of a model layout. In earlier years Ilfracombe trains were obliged to attach an additional brake van at this point. (Ilfracombe Museum)

Braunton	**1928**	**1936**
No. of passenger tickets issued	40213	22175
No. of season tickets issued	66	110
No. of tickets collected	49227	31835
No. of telegrams	704	2312
Parcels forwarded	4851	5253
Parcels received	8561	12683
Horses forwarded	22	-
Milk forwarded - cans 1928/gallons 1936	-	1807
Milk received - cans 1928/gallons 1936	-	1231
General goods forwarded (tons)	1401	1629
General goods received (tons)	2677	2777
Coal, Coke etc.	1822	3067
Other minerals forwarded	567	346
Other minerals received	2668	3290
Trucks livestock forwarded	11	80
Trucks livestock received	20	11
Lavatory pennies	528	446

52. No. 34106 *Lydford* ambles in with four coaches bound for Ilfracombe on 12th July 1963. Clean platforms were still commonplace but clean engines were becoming a rarity. (T.Wright)

54. "Braunton for Saunton Sands and Croyde Bay" announces the running-in board. The area is noted for its beautiful scenic coastline. Also evident are the water column by the signal box (there was another behind the camera) and the curved roof on the water tank. (A.F.E.Field)

53. A few minutes later the same train departs and immediately runs onto a 1 in 76 gradient which steepens greatly on the six mile climb to Mortehoe, while a passenger takes an illegal short cut. The train obscures the bankers siding. (T.Wright)

55. On the left of the previous photograph is part of the goods shed which is shown more fully here, albeit after the end of goods services which were withdrawn on 7th September 1964. The shed was later converted to serve as a youth club. (Wessex coll.)

56. The up platform waiting shelter is shown in detail, partly for the benefit of modellers. The reason for the main buildings being on the side with the least departing traffic is not known. (Wessex coll.)

57. The signal box had 24 levers, three of which were spare, and a gate wheel. It became a ground frame when the down line was taken out of use on 17th December 1967. The up line was abandoned north of the crossover seen in picture 53. (Wessex coll.)

58.   By 1993 the level crossing had been replaced by a pedestrian crossing, the platform area was occupied by a health centre and car park, while the station house had become a shop. A population increase from 2600 in 1921 to 6400 in 1971 did little to improve rail revenue as the buses were more frequent and cheaper. (V.Mitchell)

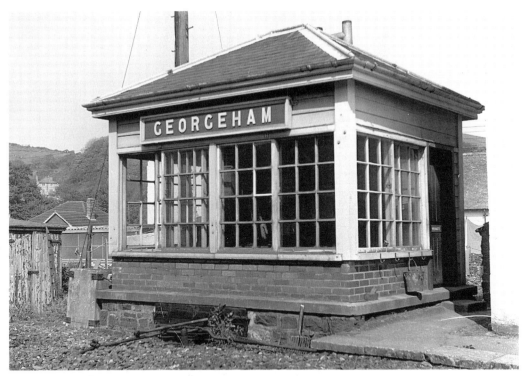

59. A five-lever frame was in use at George-ham Crossing which was less than a half mile from Braunton. The track from there to Mortehoe was doubled on 1st July 1889 and this and the other boxes on the section were opened at this time. (Wessex coll.)

60. Stoney Bridge gate box had six levers but only five were used. It was situated nearly two miles from Braunton. (Wessex coll.)

61. Heddon Mill and Willingcott were the other two boxes in this section demanding staff and running costs. Resident keepers in adjacent cottages helped to reduce this but removal of the up line (foreground) did not. (Wessex coll.)

←

62. Heddon Mills knee frame was typical of the installations of the period. On the left is the train register which had to be completed meticulously in ink for regular inspection. Unlike the other three boxes, Heddon Mill was a block post, and it also worked a trailing crossover until about 1922. (Wessex coll.)

MORTEHOE & WOOLACOMBE

63. The spelling was MORTHOE until 13th May 1902. This village was nearly two miles from the station, down steep narrow lanes as were Woolacombe and Lee. The 53 yd long down siding west is in the distance - it remained usable until 1965. (Lens of Sutton)

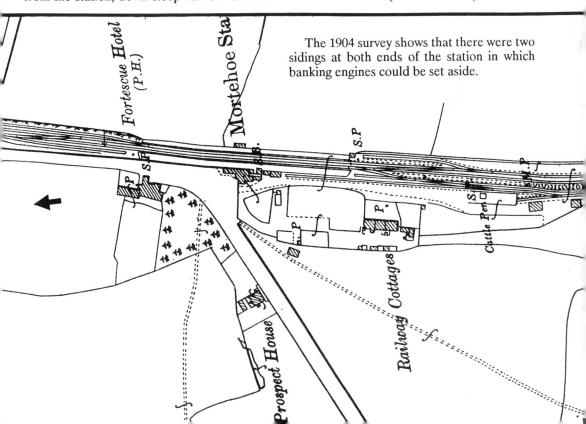

The 1904 survey shows that there were two sidings at both ends of the station in which banking engines could be set aside.

64. Class M7 no. E30 is probably seen sometime before 1931 when the former LSWR fleet began to loose their E (for Eastleigh) prefix. In the background is up siding west which was removed in the 1950s.
(Lens of Sutton)

65. A southward view includes the crane (25 cwt capacity) and the small goods yard which closed on 7th September 1964. The 1 in 40 gradient up from the south ends by the signals, 1 in 288 continuing up through the platforms.
(A.F.E.Field)

66. The 2.55pm Saturdays only Ilfracombe to Waterloo was piloted up the bank by class N No. 31844 on 25th June 1960, although consisting of only three coaches and two vans. A lower quadrant signal and a concrete post were unusual by that time. (N.L.Browne)

Mortehoe	1928	1936
No. of passenger tickets issued	20806	11553
No. of season tickets issued	99	71
No. of tickets collected	52145	29698
No. of telegrams	811	706
Parcels forwarded	1356	1026
Parcels received	6548	7800
Horses forwarded	7	21
Milk forwarded - cans 1928/gallons 1936	-	10
Milk received - cans 1928/gallons 1936	290	4596
General goods forwarded (tons)	188	299
General goods received (tons)	2055	1450
Coal, Coke etc.	1449	1770
Other minerals forwarded	6	-
Other minerals received	1270	994
Trucks livestock forwarded	23	15
Trucks livestock received	7	-
Lavatory pennies	2664	1473

67. The station was officially "Mortehoe and Woolacombe" from 5th June 1950. The combined populations were 305 in 1871, 1515 in 1921 and down to 1261 in 1971. In the summer holidays these figures increased enormously. (J.Scrace)

68. Up siding east and the shunting bell box flank no. 34070 *Manston* on 9th Sepember 1963 while it works the 10.30am from Ilfracombe. This locomotive was subject to a prolonged restoration programme at Richborough, not many miles from the Kent RAF station after which it was named. (J.Scrace)

69. The box had 20 levers (4 were spare) and was built during the track doubling operation. This was completed from here to Ilfracombe on 1st July 1891. The flat roofed goods shed appears to be of SR origin. (Wessex coll.)

70. The station suffered a bad start with a severe fire on 13th August 1874, within a month of opening. Apart from SR additions there were no other changes of note. Until about 1925, down trains waited here for all tickets to be collected. (Wessex coll.)

71.   Three railway clubs ran this special train on the last day of operation, 3rd October 1970. The final train was the 19.55 from Ilfracombe, an eight-car DMU formation carrying over 500 passengers. (S.C.Nash)

72.   The rivetted steel faced canopy construction was an early SR feature and so presumably dates from that company's era of branch line improvements. The summit of the line can be seen under the road bridge. (Wessex coll.)

73. A July 1993 photograph reveals that the buildings and canopies have been incorporated into a children's theme park, "Once upon a time", developed in 1987. The platforms, a lamp and the nameboard posts have also survived. (V.Mitchell)

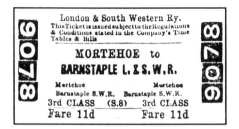

74. A northward view of the down platform may give the impression that the last train was hijacked. In reality they are BR Mk. I coaches, one of which contains representations of fairy tales and the other houses old pier machines. (V.Mitchell)

MORTEHOE BANK

There now follows a number of views of trains on the steep gradients both sides of Mortehoe. This section is a tribute to the locomen who toiled against gravity on these arduous climbs and it is best read, for full enjoyment, whilst playing a recording of locomotives working against severe gradients.

75. The leading carriage is of interest in this photo from about 1928. It is a GWR single ended slip coach which would have started from Paddington on the "Cornish Riviera" and been slipped while the express sped west near Taunton. It would then be attached to a local train to Barnstaple and transferred to this SR train at Barnstaple Junction. An N class is at the head. (R.S.Carpenter coll.)

77. Ex-SR 2-6-0 no. 31834 is piloting ex-GWR 0-6-0 no. 2268 on a northbound train in 1950. There were two through trains on weekdays from Taunton that summer, arriving at Ilfracombe at 8.26am and 3.56pm. (C.R.L.Coles)

76. No. 34010 *Sidmouth* meets no. 34006 *Bude* near the summit in the summer of 1950. The latter locomotive was one of only three to have extended smoke deflectors. After rebuilding, the "West Country" and "Battle of Britain" classes were too heavy for the route. (C.R.L.Coles)

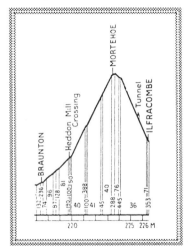

78. N class no. 31849 has steam to spare as it pilots one of its sisters up the stiff climb on 16th August 1958. Various passengers enjoy the music. (A.E.Bennett)

79. The "Ian Allan Railtour" on 19th October 1963 was hauled by nos. 7332 and 7317 and banked by N class no. 31840. No. 4472 *Flying* *Scotsman* hauled the train from Paddington to Taunton and from Exeter Central to Waterloo. (S.C.Nash)

80. Ex-GWR no. 6326 of the 4300 class approaches Mortehoe with the 10.12am Ilfracombe to Cardiff service on 29th August 1964. The train ran via Weston-super-Mare General (2.17pm) and arrived at Cardiff General at 4.18pm. (S.C.Nash)

81. No. 34042 *Dorchester* was working seven coaches unassisted to Ilfracombe when pictured in the summer of 1950. This was also the maximum permitted load for an N class. (C.R.L.Coles)

82. Drifting down the gradient on 29th August 1964 is no. 6363 with the 8.30am Taunton to Ilfracombe working. In the previous summer there had been five such through workings, but on Saturdays only. (S.C.Nash)

83. The gradient post near Mortehoe heralded one of the steepest double track sections of railway in the country. (J.Scrace)

84. Passing in the steep sided valley on 24th June 1960 is no. 34107 *Blandford Forum* and an unrecorded N class. Clear exhaust indicates perfect combustion. (N.L.Browne)

85. Owing to the friable nature of the fissured and bedded limestone evident here, a 66yd long tunnel was constructed to avoid the problems of a deep cutting. A second bore was made for the doubling of 1891. (J.Scrace)

86. The evening sunlight was ideal for recording no. 31843 piloting no. 5336 on the 6.50pm Ilfracombe to Taunton. The up tunnel was the first and last in use. (S.C.Nash)

87. No. 34080 *74 Squadron* glides past Slade Reservoir with the Ilfracombe portion of the 11.00am departure from Waterloo on 13th September 1963. This was the "Atlantic Coast Express" (ACE) which also conveyed coaches to Padstow at that time. Earlier it was famed for having coaches for nine destinations - Ilfracombe, Torrington, Padstow, Bude, Plymouth, Exmouth, Seaton, Sidmouth and a restaurant car shed at Exeter Central. The name was introduced on 19th July 1926 and discontinued permanently on 5th September 1964, although it was dropped temporarily during WWII. (J.Scrace)

88. Slade Reservoir makes a scenic background for Hymek type 35 diesel no. D7097 as it works the 12.00 noon Ilfracombe to Waterloo on 29th August 1964. Full dieselisation took place in the following month. (S.C.Nash)

89. The Ilfracombe fixed distant was on one of the many severe curves that added to the problems of working the 1 in 36 gradient. Many were of only 15 chain radius. (J.Scrace)

90. Here is the reason why some drivers of down trains feared that they might drop off the edge of the world. From this viewpoint the station appeared to be on a small shelf and the town was invisible. (N.L.Browne)

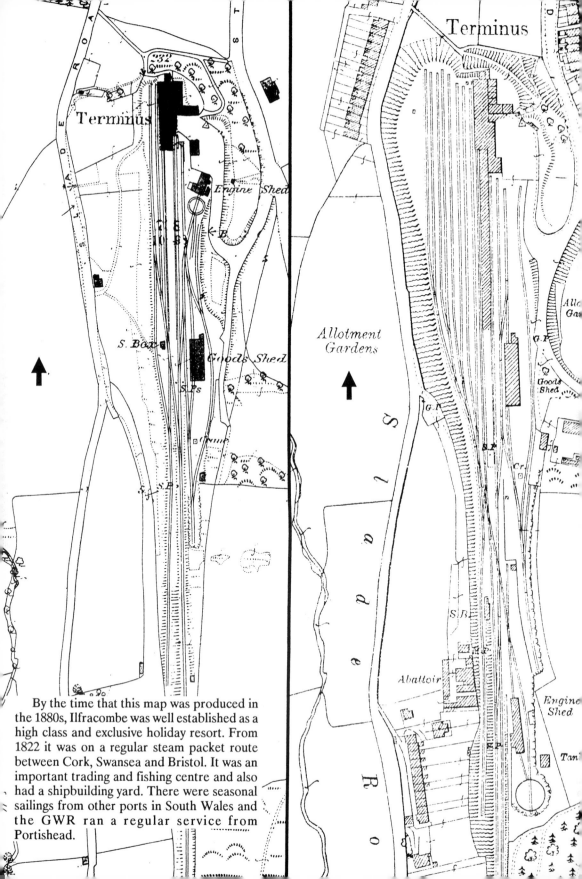

Terminus

Terminus

Engine Shed

S. Box

Goods Shed

Allotment Gardens

Goods Shed

Abattoir

Engine Shed

By the time that this map was produced in the 1880s, Ilfracombe was well established as a high class and exclusive holiday resort. From 1822 it was on a regular steam packet route between Cork, Swansea and Bristol. It was an important trading and fishing centre and also had a shipbuilding yard. There were seasonal sailings from other ports in South Wales and the GWR ran a regular service from Portishead.

ILFRACOMBE

The 1930 survey shows the extent to which the platform and adjacent tracks were lengthened and the new position for the engine shed and turntable. The population of the town (to the nearest 1000) was 5000 in 1871, 12000 in 1921 and 10000 in 1971.

91. An early view from Cairn Top shows the original track plan, with the goods shed nearest to the camera. The steeply inclined approach road is evident, the station being 254 ft above sea level. (Lens of Sutton)

ILFRACOMBE.

The shunting of coaching stock by means of gravitation on the incline at Ilfracombe station is strictly prohibited.

Goods vehicles must not be drawn on to the incline on the running line during shunting operations, unless such a course is absolutely necessary. When this arrangement must, of necessity, be resorted to, a braked vehicle must be attached at the station end of the wagons and a man provided to ride on such vehicle and apply the brake in case of emergency.

92. The track layout was planned on the basis of the short train lengths of the era. With engine power and holiday traffic demands increasing, the SR embarked upon a complete rearrangement. The LSWR salmon pink and brown coaches are behind class M7 0-4-4T no. 22. (Lens of Sutton)

93. Snow added to the difficulties of operating the branch and drifts closed the line on several occasions, notably 1891, 1947 and 1963. (Lens of Sutton)

94. Inclement weather in the form of westerly gales caused problems on the exposed platform, necessitating the erection of this shelter in about 1892. (Ilfracombe Museum)

Ilfracombe Town Office (Opened May 1930)	1932	1936
No. of passenger tickets issued	2451	2263
No. of season tickets issued	82	103
No. of tickets collected	-	-
No. of telegrams	1246	1005
Parcels forwarded	1149	1080

95.   The GWR and the LSWR both established ticket offices in the town. The LSWR's was at 97 High Street (left), next door to the local tour operator's office. The SR opened an office in May 1930 at 138 High Street. It was still in use by BR in 1960. (Ilfracombe Museum)

96.   Class M7 no. 251 departs with four coaches and bears the headcode used on many other LSWR branches. The SR later provided a larger goods crane. (R.S.Carpenter coll.)

97.   The SR completed major track improvements in May 1929. The number of carriage sidings (left) was increased from three to seven and the goods siding on the extreme right was lengthened over the site of the former engine shed. (Lens of Sutton)

98.   Driver W.H.Roulston JP was mayor of
Ilfracombe in 1935. No. 1407 was a 2-6-0 of
class N, built at Ashford Works in 1933 and
withdrawn 30 years later. (Wessex coll.)

99.   Seen on 1st September 1947, SR no. 21C146 was only one year old and was in the next year renumbered by BR to 34046. It carried the name *Braunton* and, after withdrawal in 1965 and a long period in a breakers yard, returned to Brighton, its birthplace. (S.C.Nash)

100.   Standing at the lengthened platforms in August 1953 is ex-GWR 2-6-0 no. 6372 of the 4300 class. An integrated working arrangement in 1950 resulted in more former GWR engines running on the route. (R.S.Carpenter coll.)

101. The goods yard headshunt (left) was laid in a deep excavation in 1929, the material providing fill on which to lay the additional carriage sidings. This September 1956 view includes the crane which was recorded in the 1938 handbook as being of 10-ton capacity. (H.C.Casserley)

102. The reason for the need of additional vans in holiday periods is now apparent as scouts wait to board a train home on 16th August 1958, generally regarded as the peak month for traffic in the history of the railways in the West Country. (A.E.Bennett)

Ilfracombe	1928	1936
No. of passenger tickets issued	69218	23943
No. of season tickets issued	44	448
No. of tickets collected	151641	98929
No. of telegrams	3480	2464
Parcels forwarded	6669	4054
Parcels received	54572	53307
Horses forwarded	1	61
Milk forwarded - cans 1928/gallons 1936	-	-
Milk received - cans 1928/gallons 1936	1797	15423
General goods forwarded (tons)	1265	1075
General goods received (tons)	7026	6753
Coal, Coke etc.	1474	4419
Other minerals forwarded	387	463
Other minerals received	2232	1992
Trucks livestock forwarded	8	-
Trucks livestock received	30	-
Lavatory pennies	2760	4459

103. Simmering in the sun on 2nd July 1960 are no. 34065 *Hurricane* with the 10.30am to Waterloo and no. 7319 heading the 11.00 to Wolverhampton. Arrival would be 3.53pm at Waterloo, the ACE not stopping at Barnstaple Junction on Saturdays. (N.L.Browne)

104. Local taxi firms were extremely busy on summer Saturdays, particularly in the 1950s. Between the wars the SR operated a bus service from here to Combe Martin. (Lens of Sutton)

105. The wind break (right) seems to have been largely for the benefit of locomotive crews although it would have reduced the amount of smoke and coal dust blown onto passengers. The wind was once reputed to have spun an N class locomotive on the turntable for nine hours uncontrollably. (A.F.E.Field)

106. The 1929 locomotive shed was built with concrete blocks on excavated ground, direct access to the 65ft turntable being through the shed. On the left is no. 6327 and no. 31843 is in the shed. The table was removed on 26th October 1964. (S.C.Nash)

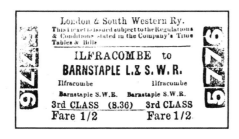

107. Shunting was undertaken by any engine that was to hand, even if it weighed almost 90 tons. This is no. 34079 *141 Squadron*, recorded in April 1964. There were seven sidings in addition to the loop. (C.L.Caddy coll.)

SOUTHERN RAILWAY.
This ticket is issued subject to the Company's
Bye-laws, Regulations & Conditions in their
Time Tables, Notices and Book of Regulations.

REVISED FARE

Ilfracombe to

25/- Waterloo   Ilfracombe
                      Waterloo

WATERLOO

| Third Class | Third Class |
| Fare 25/3 | Fare 25/- |

0405 ... 0405

SOUTHERN RAILWAY.
This ticket is issued subject to the Company's
Bye-laws, Regulations & Conditions in their
Time Tables, Notices and Book of Regulations.

Ilfracombe to

Ilfracombe   Ilfracombe
Weston S.M.   Weston S.M.

WESTON SUPER MARE
Via Barnstaple & G.W.Ry.

| Third Class | Third Class |
| Fare 11/- | Fare 11/- |

7369 ... 7369

108. Both lines in the foreground could be used to the turntable, to both platform roads and to all eight carriage sidings. The pointer on

the water gauge is at the bottom, indicating
that the tank is full. (J.Scrace)

109.   Platform lighting by electricity was
provided in 1929, the lamps being on the far
side of the posts and current being supplied
through overhead wires. No. 34072 *257
Squadron* waits to depart at 10.00am on 15th
September 1963 while other green trains stand
in the sidings. (J.Scrace)

110.   Peace prevails on the platform on 9th September 1963 as the peak holiday season is just over. The electric lighting on no. 34070 *Manston* is clearly visible as it waits with the 10.30am departure for Waterloo. (J.Scrace)

112.   With another locomotive at the other end, class N no. 31837 hauls empty ex-LMS stock out of platform 2 while acting as station pilot on 25th July 1964. At busy times the longer platform 2 would be used for arrivals and no. 1 for departures. (J.H.Aston)

111.   Staff attend to a gleaming set of Bulleid coaches on 25th July 1964 while no. 31837 acts as station pilot and a diesel waits to be released. Steam was doomed and would be extinct here within two months. (J.H.Aston)

113. A few minutes later the stock passes the signal box and it becomes apparent that the train engine had been sister engine no. 31406. The headcode indicates that the train had run via Taunton. (J.H.Aston)

114. More ex-LMS stock is evident as we look up the valley onto the side of which the station was built. The siding behind the signal box is level and terminates close to the abattoir. The box had 50 levers but 10 were never used. (Wessex coll.)

GOODS OFFICE

115.   For many years the up freight was scheduled to depart at 2.25pm, call at Mortehoe (2.39 to 3.23), Braunton (3.40 to 4.11), Wrafton (4.14 to 4.29) and to arrive at Barnstaple Junction at 4.43pm. This class of engine (N) was limited to 15 loaded wagons and a van, but if pulling over 11 trucks it was required to have two manned brake vans. (Wessex coll.)

116.   Goods facilities were withdrawn on 7th September 1964 and the sidings were lifted in 1966, but those to the engine shed had gone in 1964. (Wessex coll.)

117.   Removal of signalling was in progress on 30th July 1969, although the box had closed on 17th December 1967 when the arms would have been removed. (D.Aston)

118. The carriage sidings were taken out of use when the box closed, with the exception of one which remained until the following year. Ground frames were installed at each end of the loop which is seen in April 1970. (S.C.Nash)

119. This is the 15.28 departure on 29th April 1970. At this period only one Saturday evening train gave a direct service to Exeter Central, the station near the shops and destination for most local travellers. (S.C.Nash)

3rd SINGLE   SINGLE 3rd

Mortehoe & Woolacombe to
Mortehoe & W.   Mortehoe & W
Ilfracombe   Ilfracombe
ILFRACOMBE
(W)   7d.   FARE 7d.   (W)
ForConditions see over ForConditions see over

120. The ground frame is at the end of the shelter and a class 118 DMU (no. W51322 leading) is at the end of the line, in both senses. It is working the 15.28 to Exeter on the last day of operation, 3rd October 1970. The last through train had been on 26th September of that year and was hauled by no. D810 *Cockade*. It was the 13.55 (Saturdays only) to Paddington, eight coaches plus a restaurant car. (D.Mitchell)

MP **Middleton Press**

Easebourne Lane, Midhurst, West Sussex GU29 9AZ
Tel: (0730) 813169   Fax: (0730) 812601

Companion albums in this style for other West of England lines

Branch Lines ...

Branch Lines to Exmouth
Branch Line to Lyme Regis
Branch Line to Lynton
Branch Line to Minehead
Branch Lines to Seaton and Sidmouth
Branch Line to Swanage to 1992
Branch Lines around Weymouth
(Abbotsbury, Easton and The Quay Tramway)

Southern Main Lines ...

Exeter to Barnstaple
Salisbury to Yeovil
Yeovil to Exeter

Country Railway Routes ...

Bath to Evercreech Junction
Bournemouth to Evercreech Junction
Burnham to Evercreech Junction
Yeovil to Dorchester
(including the Bridport Branch)

Write or telephone for the full list of Southern Classics